Practical
Pasta Sauces

p^3

This is a P³ Book
First published in 2003

P³
Queen Street House
4 Queen Street
Bath BA1 1HE, UK

ISBN: 1-40540-924-X

Printed in China

NOTE

This book uses metric and imperial measurements. Follow the same units
of measurement throughout; do not mix metric and imperial.
All spoon measurements are level: teaspoons are assumed to be 5 ml, and
tablespoons are assumed to be 15 ml. Unless otherwise stated,
milk is assumed to be full fat, eggs and individual vegetables such as potatoes
are medium, and pepper is freshly ground black pepper.

The nutritional information provided for each recipe is per serving or per person.
Optional ingredients, variations or serving suggestions have
not been included in the calculations. The times given for each recipe are an approximate
guide only because the preparation times may differ according to the techniques used by
different people and the cooking times may vary as a result of the type of oven used.

Recipes using raw or very lightly cooked eggs should be
avoided by children, the elderly, pregnant women, convalescents,
and anyone suffering from an illness.

Contents

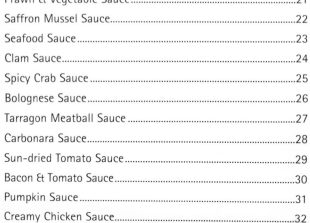

Introduction

Creative cooks will enjoy partnering their favourite sauces with a variety of pastas. Although there are classic combinations, such as Spaghetti Bolognese (see page 26) and Spaghetti Carbonara (see page 28), there are no rules, just guidelines, which are largely a matter of practicality, appearance and taste. When you have tried the delicious sauce recipes featured in this book, you might like to try exciting new combinations of pastas and sauces. Long ribbons and round pasta give tomato-based and oil-based sauces something to cling to, while shaped pastas and hollow tubes are ideal for trapping chunkier sauces in their crevices.

Pasta shapes

Here are the main pasta shapes you are likely to find in your local supermarket or delicatessen:

Anelli, anellini, anelletti small rings used for soup
Bavette, bavettini thin, oval tubes
Bigoli wholewheat pasta from the Veneto
Bozzoli deeply-ridged, cocoon-like shapes
Brichetti 'small bricks'
Bucatini long, medium-thick tubes
Cappelletti wide-brimmed hat shapes
Capelli d'angelo angel's hair pasta, thinner than capellini
Capellini fine strands of ribbon pasta
Casareccia short, curled lengths of pasta from Sicily, twisted at one end
Cavatappi short, thick corkscrew shapes
Chifferi, chifferini, chifferotti small, curved tubes
Conchiglie ridged shells
Conchigliette little shells used for soup
Corallini small rings

Cornetti ridged shells
Cravatte, cravattini bows
Creste di galli 'cock's comb', curved shapes
Dischi volante 'flying saucers'
Ditali, ditalini 'little thimbles', short tubes
Eliche loose, spiral shapes
Elicoidali short, ridged tubes
Farfalle bows

Fedeli, fedelini fine tubes twisted into skeins
Festonati short lengths, like festoons
Fettucine narrow ribbon pasta
Fiochette, fiochelli small bows
Frezine broad, flat ribbons
Fusilli spindles or short spirals
Fusilli bucati thin spirals, like springs
Gemelli 'twins', two pieces wrapped together
Gramigna 'grass' or 'weed', look like sprouting seeds; from Emilia Romagna
Lasagne flat, rectangular sheets
Linguine long, flat ribbons
Lumache smooth, snail-like shells
Lumachine U-shaped flat pasta
Macaroni, maccheroni long- or short-cut tubes, may be ridged or elbow-shaped
Maltagliati triangular
Orecchiette ear-shaped
Orzo tiny, rice-like grains
Pappardelle widest ribbons, straight with saw-tooth edges
Pearlini tiny discs
Penne 'quills', short, thick tubes with diagonally cut ends
Pipe rigate ridged, curved pipe shapes
Rigatoni thick, ridged tubes
Rotelle wheels
Ruote wheels

Buttered Pea & Cheese Sauce

This delicious sauce is served with *paglia e fieno* ('straw and hay' pasta), which refers to the colours of the pasta when mixed together.

NUTRITIONAL INFORMATION

Calories	 699	Sugars	.... 7g
Protein	.... 26g	Fat	.... 39g
Carbohydrate	... 65g	Saturates	...... 23g

 10 mins   10 mins

SERVES 4

INGREDIENTS

450 g/1 lb mixed fresh green and white
  spaghetti or tagliatelle

shavings of Parmesan cheese, to garnish

SAUCE

4 tbsp butter

450 g/1 lb fresh peas, shelled

200 ml/7 fl oz double cream

55 g/2 oz Parmesan cheese, freshly grated

pinch of freshly grated nutmeg

salt and pepper

1 To make the sauce, melt the butter in a large saucepan. Add the peas and cook over a low heat for 2–3 minutes.

2 Pour 150 ml/5 fl oz of the cream into the pan, bring to the boil and then simmer for 1–1½ minutes or until slightly thickened. Remove the pan from the heat.

3 Meanwhile, to cook the pasta, bring a large saucepan of lightly salted water to the boil. Add the pasta, bring back to the boil and cook for 2–3 minutes or until just tender but still firm to the bite. Remove the pan from the heat, drain the pasta thoroughly and return to the pan.

4 Add the sauce to the pasta. Return the pan to the heat and add the

remaining cream and the Parmesan cheese. Season to taste with nutmeg and salt and pepper.

5 While heating through, use 2 forks to toss the pasta gently so that it is coated with the sauce.

6 Transfer the pasta to a warmed serving dish and serve immediately, garnished with Parmesan shavings.

VARIATION

Cook 140 g/5 oz sliced button or oyster mushrooms in about 4 tablespoons of butter over a low heat for 4–5 minutes. Stir into the sauce just before adding to the pasta in step 4.

Chilli & Red Pepper Sauce

This roasted red pepper and chilli sauce is sweet and spicy – the perfect combination for those who like to add just a little spice to life!

NUTRITIONAL INFORMATION

Calories	423	Sugars	.........5g
Protein	.........9g	Fat	..........27g
Carbohydrate	...38g	Saturates	.......4g

25 mins   30 mins

SERVES 4

INGREDIENTS

675 g/1 lb 8 oz fresh pasta or 350 g/12 oz dried pasta

fresh oregano leaves, to garnish

SAUCE

2 red peppers, halved and deseeded

1 small, fresh, red chilli

4 tomatoes, halved

2 garlic cloves

55 g/2 oz ground almonds

100 ml/3½ fl oz olive oil

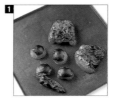  

1 To make the sauce, place the red peppers, skin side up, on a baking sheet with the chilli and tomatoes. Cook under a preheated grill for 15 minutes until charred. After 10 minutes, turn the tomatoes over, skin side up. Put the peppers and chillies in a plastic bag and set aside for 10 minutes.

2 Peel the skins from the red peppers and chilli and slice the flesh into strips. Peel the garlic, and peel and deseed the tomato halves.

3 Place the ground almonds on a baking sheet and place under the grill for 2–3 minutes until golden.

4 In a food processor, process the red peppers, chilli, garlic and tomatoes to make a purée. With the motor still running, slowly add the olive oil through the feeder tube to form a thick sauce. Alternatively, mash the mixture with a fork and beat in the olive oil, drop by drop.

5 Stir the toasted ground almonds into the mixture. Warm the sauce in a pan until it is heated through.

6 To cook the pasta, bring a large saucepan of lightly salted water to the boil. Add the pasta, bring back to the boil and cook for 3–5 minutes if using fresh pasta or 8–10 minutes if using dried pasta. Drain well and transfer to a serving dish. Pour over the sauce and toss to mix. Garnish with the fresh oregano leaves and serve.

VARIATION

Add 2 tablespoons of red wine vinegar to the sauce and use as a dressing for a cold pasta salad, if you wish.

Fragrant Aubergine Sauce

Prepare the marinated aubergines well in advance so that, when you are ready to eat, all you have to do is cook the pasta.

NUTRITIONAL INFORMATION	
Calories 378	Sugars 3g
Protein 12g	Fat 30g
Carbohydrate ...16g	Saturates 3g

12¼ hrs   15 mins

SERVES 4

INGREDIENTS

150 ml/5 fl oz vegetable stock

150 ml/5 fl oz white wine vinegar

2 tsp balsamic vinegar

3 tbsp olive oil

sprig of fresh oregano

450 g/1 lb aubergines, peeled and thinly sliced

400 g/14 oz dried linguine

MARINADE

2 tbsp extra-virgin olive oil

2 garlic cloves, crushed

2 tbsp chopped fresh oregano

2 tbsp finely chopped roasted almonds

2 tbsp diced red pepper

2 tbsp lime juice

grated rind and juice of 1 orange

salt and pepper

1 Put the vegetable stock, wine vinegar and balsamic vinegar into a saucepan and bring to the boil over a low heat. Add 2 teaspoons of the olive oil and the sprig of fresh oregano and simmer gently for about 1 minute.

2 Add the aubergine slices to the pan, remove from the heat and set aside for 10 minutes.

3 Meanwhile, to make the marinade, combine the oil, garlic, fresh oregano, almonds, red pepper, lime juice, and orange rind and juice in a large bowl and season to taste with salt and pepper.

4 Using a slotted spoon, carefully remove the aubergine slices from the pan and drain well. Add the aubergine to the marinade, mixing well to coat. Cover with clingfilm and set aside in the refrigerator for about 12 hours.

5 To cook the pasta, bring a large saucepan of lightly salted water to the boil. Add half of the remaining oil and the linguine. Bring back to the boil and cook for 8–10 minutes until just tender but still firm to the bite.

6 Drain the pasta thoroughly and toss with the remaining oil while it is still warm. Arrange the pasta on a serving plate with the aubergine slices and the marinade and serve immediately.

Tuna & Anchovy Sauce

The delicious parsley sauce in this recipe enhances the classic Italian combination of pasta and tuna.

NUTRITIONAL INFORMATION	
Calories 1065	Sugars 3g
Protein 27g	Fat 85g
Carbohydrate ... 52g	Saturates 18g

10 mins   15 mins

SERVES 4

INGREDIENTS

450 g/1 lb dried spaghetti

1 tbsp olive oil

2 tbsp butter

stoned black olives, to garnish

warm crusty bread, to serve

SAUCE

200 g/7 oz canned tuna, drained

60 g/2¼ oz canned anchovies, drained

225 ml/8 fl oz olive oil

60 g/2¼ oz flat-leaved parsley, coarsely chopped, plus extra to garnish

150 ml/5 fl oz crème fraîche

salt and pepper

1 To make the sauce, remove any bones from the tuna. Put the tuna into a food processor or blender. Add the anchovies, oil and parsley. Process until very smooth.

2 Spoon the crème fraîche into the food processor or blender and process again for a few seconds to blend thoroughly. Season with salt and pepper to taste.

3 To cook the pasta, bring a large saucepan of lightly salted water to the boil. Add the spaghetti and olive oil and cook for 8–10 minutes or until tender but still firm to the bite.

4 Drain the spaghetti, return to the pan and place over a medium heat. Add the butter and toss well to coat. Spoon in the sauce and quickly toss into the spaghetti, mixing well using 2 forks.

5 Remove the pan from the heat and divide the spaghetti between warm individual serving plates. Garnish with olives and parsley and serve with warm, crusty bread.

VARIATION

If desired, you could add 1–2 garlic cloves to the sauce substitute 25 g/1 oz chopped fresh basil for half the parsley, and garnish with capers instead of black olives.

  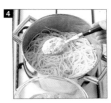

Sun-dried Tomato Sauce

There is an appetizing contrast of textures and flavours in this satisfying sauce, which is an excellent accompaniment for meatballs and pasta.

NUTRITIONAL INFORMATION

Calories 910   Sugars 13g
Protein . . . . .40g   Fat 54g
Carbohydrate . . .65g   Saturates 19g

45 mins   1 hr 5 mins

SERVES 4

INGREDIENTS

500 g/1 lb 2 oz minced lean beef

55 g/2 oz soft white breadcrumbs

1 garlic clove, crushed

2 tbsp chopped fresh parsley

1 tsp dried oregano

pinch of freshly grated nutmeg

¼ tsp ground coriander

55 g/2 oz Parmesan cheese, freshly grated

2–3 tbsp milk

plain flour, for dusting

3 tbsp olive oil

400 g/14 oz dried tagliatelle

2 tbsp butter, diced

fresh salad leaves, to serve

SAUCE

3 tbsp olive oil

2 large onions, sliced

2 celery sticks, thinly sliced

2 garlic cloves, chopped

400 g/14 oz canned chopped tomatoes

125 g/4½ oz sun-dried tomatoes in oil, drained and chopped

2 tbsp tomato purée

1 tbsp dark muscovado sugar

about 150 ml/5 fl oz white wine or water

salt and pepper

1 To make the sauce, heat the oil in a frying pan. Add the onions and celery and cook until translucent. Add the garlic and cook for 1 minute. Stir in all the tomatoes, tomato purée, sugar, and wine or water, and season to taste with salt and pepper. Bring to the boil and simmer for 10 minutes.

2 Meanwhile, break up the meat in a bowl with a wooden spoon until it becomes a sticky paste. Stir in the breadcrumbs, garlic, herbs and spices. Stir in the cheese and enough milk to make a firm paste. Flour your hands, take large spoonfuls of the mixture and shape it into 12 balls. Heat the oil in a frying pan and cook the meatballs for 5–6 minutes until browned.

3 Pour the tomato sauce over the meatballs. Lower the heat, cover the pan and simmer for 30 minutes, turning once or twice. Add a little extra wine or water if the sauce is beginning to become dry.

4 To cook the pasta, bring a large saucepan of lightly salted water to the boil. Add the pasta, bring back to the boil and cook for 8–10 minutes until tender but still firm to the bite. Drain, turn into a warmed serving dish, dot with the butter and toss with 2 forks. Spoon the meatballs and sauce over the pasta and serve immediately with fresh salad leaves.